The Sockosaurus

A play by Julia Donaldson
Illustrated by Aleksei Bitskoff

Characters

Sockosaurus

Father C
(Father Christmas)

Father C: Hurry up, deer! We're late.

Deer 1: But I'm hungry.

Deer 2: So am I.

Deer 3: I'm sleepy.

Deer 4: Me too.

Father C: Stop moaning. Look! A roof!

Deer 1: At last!

Father C: Slow down, we're landing.

Deer 2: But look!

Deer 3: Who's that in the chimney?

Father C: Yes, who are you?

Sockosaurus: I'm a Sockosaurus!

Deer 4: What's a Sockosaurus?

Deer 2: And what is he doing in the chimney?

Father C: Yes, what are you doing in the chimney?

Sockosaurus: I'm trying to get down it.

Father C: But that's my job.

Sockosaurus: No, it's not. It's my job!

Deer 3: Why do you want to go down chimneys?

Sockosaurus: So I can eat socks.

Deer 1: What socks?

Sockosaurus: The socks that the children hang out for me.

Deer 4: They don't hang them out for you!

Deer 2: No. They are for Father Christmas.

Father C: Yes! I fill them with presents.

Sockosaurus: Well, **I'm** still going to eat them!

Deer 2: Oh no you're not!

Sockosaurus: Oh yes I am!

Deer 3: Oh no you're not!

Sockosaurus: Oh yes I am!

Deer 1: Oh no you're not!

Sockosaurus: Well, if you won't let me eat socks, I'll have to eat deer …

Deer 4: Help!

Deer 2: We'll fly away!

Sockosaurus: I can fly faster.

Father C: Can you really fly?

Sockosaurus: You bet!

Father C: And are you strong?

Sockosaurus: Yes!

Father C: I have a plan.

Sockosaurus: I hope it's a good one.

Deer 3: What is it, Father Christmas?

Deer 1: Tell us!

Father C: Well, back at home I have lots of socks. I get ten pairs from my granny every Christmas, and I never wear them.

Sockosaurus: Yummy!

Father C: If you help pull the sleigh tonight, you can eat all my socks.

Sockosaurus: Can I have deer for pudding?

Deer 1: No!

Deer 4: Help!

Father C: No, you can't. But if you are good you can eat all my ties too.

Sockosaurus: Yummy! Let's start now!